COOKING UP A CONVERSATION

BY   CHEF CARL REDDING AND CHEF DANA PATTERSON

WORLD RENOWNED AND TRENDING

Copyright ©2018

COOKING UP A CONVERSATION

BY CHEF CARL REDDING AND CHEF DANA PATTERSON

WORLD RENOWNED AND TRENDING

Printed in the United States of America
ISBN 978-0-9990755-5-5

All rights reserved solely by the authors. The authors guarantee all contents are original and do not infringe upon the legal rights of any other person or work. No part of this book may be reproduced in any form without the permission of the authors.

Back cover photo of Chef Carl Redding courtesy of Phaedra Williamson.

Carl Redding

When Elijah Bass tried to chase his grandson, Carl, out of the family kitchen in Gordon, Alabama, to toughen him up by assigning him, his brothers and his cousins outdoor chores, little could he imagine that Carl would become a US Marine *and* a baker. Nor probably did his grandmother, Amy Ruth Moore Bass, imagine that her summer sous-chef, visiting from New York, would in 1999 become Proprietor of a famous Harlem Institution named in her honor.

Chef Carl Redding grew up in the Polo Grounds Towers, a public housing project on 8th Avenue and 155th Street in Harlem, located on land where the hallowed Polo Grounds sports stadium stood before being razed in 1964.

When Carl's mother, Inez Bass, walked him and his brothers to school, Carl noted the smell of breads and other bakery items wafting down from "up on the hill." When his mother finally took him to the source of those smells, he met "Uncle" Tommy Wilson and his wife Elizabeth, the owners of Wilson's Bakery and Restaurant on 158th St. and Amsterdam Avenue. He fell in love with the place and eventually convinced the Wilsons to let him wash dishes. Within a couple of weeks, he was managing the cake counter, selling not just cakes but also biscuits, corn muffins and other delectables. From there he began decorating cakes and then baking them. But he also learned how to *really* cook on a commercial level. "I always watched and watched and watched. That's where I got the professional cooking thing from."

In the summers, he was at the Bass farm, cooking with his grandmother and canning, preserving and freezing the vegetables and fruit grown on 15 or so acres of the family's

homestead: tomatoes, green beans, field peas, okra, figs, peaches -- you name it. He shucked corn, shelled peas, gathered pecans and walnuts, milked cows and collected eggs. He also helped with slaughtering chickens, hogs and cows raised on the farm and freezing the meat. His family's goal was to be self-sufficient.

After an 8 year stint in the US Marines and nine plus years as a personal assistant and Chief of Staff to the Rev. Al Sharpton's National Action Network also noting that he helped found and shape NAN, Chef Carl answered what he knew was God telling him it was time to move on. It was time to open his own business/restaurant. With the financial investments of a number of people, including Attorney Johnnie Cochran, famed Criminal and Civil-Rights Attorney, Joseph Leake, NYPD Chief of Police, Sheila Thomas, the owner of a Harlem seafood restaurant, Percy Sutton, the political media titan, and Reggie Harris, a television newsman, he was on his way. After the backbreaking work of transforming a former restaurant that had been busted two years before in a major drug raid, Chef Carl opened Amy Ruth's on Mother's Day 1999 with 63 seats and lines of people outside his door on 116th Street. That brought out the press, and he found himself the subject of newspaper articles and features on local and national television. "I knew that God had my back."

Chef Carl has had the opportunity to personally cook for the likes of Gayle King, Oprah Winfrey, President Bill Clinton, Senator Hillary Clinton, Bishop TD Jakes, Michael Jackson, Luther Vandross, and scores of others.

Keeping himself busy, Chef Carl has enrolled into the Art Institute of Atlanta to pursue a Bachelor of Science degree in Culinary Management.

COOKING UP A CONVERSATION

Dana Patterson

Dana Patterson was the least likely to become a Certified Executive Chef. His cooking adventures started like many others, in his Grandmother's (Ruby Colson's) kitchen. Chef Dana was one of those kids who got into a lot of mischief. Nothing serious but enough for his Grandmother to say, "Since you want to be out there acting up, you can just come in here with me and help me cook."

She would always have something for him to do, and she would always make him feel very loved and comfortable in her kitchen. In that kitchen is where he learned those passed down family recipes that were rich in American- Indian and Southern culture. This later prepared him to make a smooth transition into different cooking techniques and different Cuisines. The Culinary School in Baltimore's Inner Harbor really prepared him for life as a Chef.

At the end of his Culinary School career, Chef Dana first worked with a White House Official that was having a small function for dignitaries such as Al Gore, Aretha Franklin, Al Sharpton and David Justice to name a few. That really set him up to be in the niche place which became where he would be for the next 20 years of his career. He later became what they call, the Chef to the Stars, doing a few functions for the likes of Michael Jackson, Arnold Palmer, Frankie Beverly, Gene Simmons, Riva Tims, Lisa Presley, George Clinton, Darius Rucker and Shaquille O'Neal. He would be remised if he did not mention being able to provide his Chef services for one of his favorite charity functions, Wounded Veterans at the House of Blues where celebrities such as Gary Sinise and many others attended. Later on Chef Dana became the Personal Chef to Hall of Famer, Dominique Wilkins.

Chef Dana started a Chef Placement agency after the discovery that many of his celebrity clientele moved within the same social circles and that there culinary needs and personnel would be similar. His agency placed Chefs with Hall of Famer Tracy McGrady, Hall of Famer Alonzo Mourning, Gary Sheffield, Barry Bonds, Hall of Famer Patrick Ewing, Pervis Ellison, Gerald Wilkins and David Rivers.
In 2016 Chef Dana's life took a sudden turn at the fact that he needed a below the knee amputation which he says reminded of who he is who he belonged to; his God.
He says he is blessed to be a blessing. This life altering experience caused him to reconsider priorities and forgotten dreams. One of those forgotten dreams was the undertaking of this book. His says, "I am grateful for you the reader for being a part of this chapter in my ongoing biography."

COOKING UP A CONVERSATION

Acknowledgments/Dedication

Chef Carl

I'd like to publicly acknowledge and to thank my FATHER GOD for saving my soul and for HIM to continue giving me life. Thanks Mom (Inez) for everything and all that you do to support me. Thank you Aunt Ressie Mae Bass for your support. I gotta send a thank you to my 2 brothers Gregory and Eric and Eric's wife Tracye for Yall's continued support of me.

I want to send a special thanks to my best friends in this world; April Robinson, Lesly Papailler, Chef Curtis Aiken's, Chef Brian Duhart and Edward Bosley.

Thank you Diane Harris, Joe Leake, Dr Gregory Paige, Mel Randal, and Sheila Thomas my financial crew who helped me with the building of my very 1st restaurant Amy Ruth's which still stands today in Harlem, NY. Also thank you for being a part of this crew, RIP Percy Sutton, Reggie Harris, Johnnie Cochran, and Wilhelmina Billie Holiday.

A special thanks goes out to Rev. Al Sharpton. We spent 9+ inseparable years working together. It was he who taught me and gave me my civil rights education, political chops and my master marketing and people skills.

Thanks to my spiritual fathers, brothers and mentors; Rev Jesse L Jackson, Rev Calvin O Butts, Rev Michael Walrond, Rev Christopher Bullock, Rev Alan Waller, Rev Johnnie Green, Dr Bobby Jones, Rev E Dewey Smith, Rev Raphael Warnock, Rev Shanan Jones, Bishop Aran McClary.... RIP Rev Timothy Wright, Rev James Cleveland, Rev William Agustus Jones, Rev Dr Wyatt Tee Walker

Finally I'd like to thank Pastor Sean Cort for believing in the vision of this book and for putting your money where your mouth is by being the Publisher of this wonderful cookbook.

Chef Dana

This Book is dedicated to you.
It's not by chance you're holding this book.

This book is for the person who knows it's better to walk a tight rope than to stand still on one. Keep it moving. I am grateful to the many Life-Coaches Teachers, Friends and Pastors that have sown into my life. I am thankful to my Grand-Mothers and Family, Geraldine Adams, Thomas Patterson, Tiffany, Chanel, Dante and Ruben Patterson.
I thank God and you for the privilege and honor of sharing this with you.

APPETIZERS

Carolina Cottage Granola
By Chef Dana

Ingredients
2 cups old fashioned oats
2 cups whole wheat flakes
2 cups buckwheat groats
2 cups raisins
2 cups apricots
2 cups dried cranberries
1 cup sesame seeds
1 cup pumpkin seeds
1 cup coconut
1 cup walnuts
1 cup almonds
1 cup honey
1/2 cup butter, melted
2 tablespoons zest of orange
1 teaspoon cinnamon
1 teaspoon nutmeg

Method
Preheat oven to 350 F. Combine all ingredients. Bake for 30 minutes, constantly stirring every 5-10 minutes. (Serves 12)

Tamale Bite
By Chef Dana

Ingredients

1 pound ground beef
1 pound ground lean sausage
1 cup tomato- vegetable juice
4 beaten egg
2 teaspoons garlic powder
1 teaspoon sea salt
2 tablespoon chili powder
2 cups yellow cornmeal
1/2 cup flour
1/2 teaspoon cayenne pepper
1/4 teaspoon crushed red pepper
2 teaspoons paprika
2 teaspoons cumin

SAUCE:
5 cups tomato-vegetable juice
2 teaspoons chili powder
2 teaspoons cumin
2 teaspoons sea salt

Method

Preheat oven to 350 F. Combine meats, juice and eggs, blending and mixing well. In a separate bowl, mix all dry ingredients together. Combine with meat mixture. Roll into bite size balls and place on a baking sheet. Bake for 30 minutes.

To prepare sauce, combine all ingredients in a sauce pan and bring to a boil. Place meatballs in sauce and cook for 45 minutes over medium heat.

❈ Rum Buttered-glazed Grilled ❈ Pineapple with Vanilla/Mascarpone
By Chef Dana

Ingredients

6 ounces unsalted butter
2 tablespoons light brown sugar
1/4 cup dark rum
1 pineapple peeled and sliced
1 cup mascarpone
1 vanilla bean split and seeded
1/2 cup fresh blueberries, for garnish

Method
Preheat the grill to medium.
Melt the butter, sugar and rum in a sauce pan.
Grill pineapple on both sides until golden brown. Two to three minutes per side. Spoon the Rum glaze over the pineapple.
Whisk together mascarpone and vanilla seeds. Top each slice of pineapple with a dollop of vanilla mascarpone. Garnish with blueberries.

SALADS

Quinoa Salad with Collard Greens and Goat Cheese

By Chef Carl

INGREDIENTS

- 1 bunch Collard Greens, about 1 pound
- 4 tablespoons extra-virgin olive oil
- 1 medium red onion, chopped
- 3 large cloves garlic, slivered
- 1 cup quinoa
- 1 teaspoon dry mustard
- 2 cups vegetable broth
- Salt and ground black pepper
- 12 ounces' small cremini mushrooms, stems trimmed, halved
- 4 ounces' plain goat cheese, chilled

Method

- Remove stems from Collard Greens and chop in 1/2-inch pieces. Chop leaves and set aside.

- Heat 2 tablespoons oil in a 3-quart saucepan on medium. Add onion, garlic and collard stems. Sauté until vegetables are tender, about 5 minutes. Stir in quinoa and mustard. Add broth, stir, and season with salt and pepper. Bring to a boil, cover and cook on low 15 to 20 minutes, until the liquid is absorbed. Remove from heat, uncover and let sit 20 minutes.

- Meanwhile, heat remaining oil on medium-high in a large skillet. Add mushrooms and sauté, stirring, until lightly browned, about 10 minutes. Add collard leaves and continue cooking until greens have wilted and no more liquid remains in the skillet.

- Fluff quinoa with a fork. Fold mushrooms and leaves into it. The cooked quinoa can be set aside at room temperature for several hours and then served, or reheated to warm or hot. Crumble goat cheese and scatter on top just before serving.

Roasted Carrot Salad with Arugula and Peaches

By Chef Carl

INGREDIENTS

- 1 pound carrots, peeled and cut into 2-inch lengths
- ¼ teaspoon kosher salt, more to taste
- ⅛ teaspoon ground black pepper, more to taste
- ¼ cup plus 2 tablespoons extra-virgin olive oil, more as needed
- ½ teaspoon ground cumin
- ½ tablespoon fresh lemon juice, more to taste
- 1 garlic clove, finely grated or minced
- ½ teaspoon Dijon mustard
- 3 ounces baby arugula (about 3 cups)
- 4 Peaches, cleaned, peeled, cored, and sliced
- 1 fennel bulb, thinly sliced
- ¼ cup fresh mint leaves

METHOD

- Heat oven to 425 degrees. Toss carrots with salt, pepper and 2 tablespoons oil on a rimmed baking sheet, and bake until edges are caramelized and carrots are tender, 28 to 33 minutes. Remove from oven and immediately toss with cumin. Let cool for a few minutes while you make the dressing. Carrots should be slightly warm but not hot when tossed with the greens.

- In a large bowl, whisk together lemon juice, garlic, mustard and large pinch of salt and pepper. Taste and adjust lemon juice and seasonings if necessary. Whisk in remaining 1/4 cup oil until emulsified.

- Stir carrots into dressing, then gently toss with sliced peaches, arugula, fennel and dill or mint. Serve immediately, drizzled with more olive oil.

COOKING UP A CONVERSATION

Golden Beet Salad with Cider Vinegar Dressing

By Chef Carl

INGREDIENTS

- 5 golden beets
- 1 tablespoon extra-virgin olive oil
- ¾ cup apple cider vinegar
- Sea salt
- 3 cups mâche or other tender greens
- 1 tablespoon walnut oil
- Freshly ground pepper
- ½ cup toasted walnut pieces
- ½ cup ricotta salata or fresh goat cheese

METHOD

- Preheat oven to 425 degrees.
- Rinse the beets and cut off the greens, saving them for another use. Rub the beets with the olive oil, wrap in foil and place on a baking sheet (in case they leak). Bake until you can pierce through the middle of each beet with a knife, about 1 hour. Remove from the oven and let cool.
- While the beets are cooking, gently bring the vinegar to a boil in a small saucepan over medium heat until it is reduced by a third. Remove from the heat and let cool.
- When the beets are cool, use a paring knife to remove the skins, which should peel off easily. Cut each beet into thin slices using a sharp knife. Sprinkle them with salt and toss them in the reduced vinegar.
- Toss the mâche with the walnut oil and a few grinds of pepper. Top the mâche with the beets, walnut pieces and cheese. Use a spoon to drizzle the remaining vinegar on top, as desired. Serve immediately.

Green Tomato Salad with Russian Dressing

By Chef Carl

INGREDIENTS

- 1 ¼ pounds green tomatoes, sliced 1/4 inch thick
- 1 large red beefsteak tomato, halved and sliced 1/4 inch thick
- 2 teaspoons sherry vinegar or champagne vinegar
- 1 tablespoon extra-virgin olive oil
- Salt, preferably coarse sea salt or kosher salt, and freshly ground pepper to taste
- ¼ cup Hellmann's Real Mayonnaise
- ¼ cup plain low-fat yogurt
- 2 tablespoons ketchup
- 1 tablespoon capers, rinsed and chopped
- 2 tablespoons finely chopped red onion, soaked for five minutes in cold water, drained, rinsed, and drained on paper towels optional
- 1 teaspoon finely chopped fresh parsley
- 1 hardboiled egg, cut in wedges

METHOD

- Toss together the tomatoes, vinegar and olive oil, and season to taste with salt and pepper. Line an oval or round platter with the tomato slices, overlapping them slightly and sliding in a red tomato slice at regular intervals.

- Whisk together the mayonnaise, yogurt and ketchup. Stir in the capers and red onion. Spoon the dressing over the tomatoes. Sprinkle on the parsley, garnish with hard-boiled egg wedges, and serve.

Cucumber-Watermelon Salad

By Chef Carl

INGREDIENTS

- 4 cups **watermelon**, seeded and cut into generous 1/2-inch cubes
- 3 cups Asian or English cucumbers (about 2 large cucumbers), peeled, seeded and cut into 1/2-inch cubes
- 3 ½ tablespoons fresh lime juice
- 3 tablespoons hoisin sauce
- 2 teaspoons seeded and finely diced jalapeño, or to taste
- ½ teaspoon salt, plus more to taste
- ⅓ cup chopped flat-leaf parsley
- Black pepper
- ⅓ cup coarsely chopped lightly salted pistachios

METHOD

- Combine melon and cucumber in a colander set over a medium bowl. Cover with plastic wrap and refrigerate at least 30 minutes and up to 4 hours.

- Transfer melon and cucumber to serving bowl. Whisk lime juice, hoisin sauce, jalapeño and salt in a small bowl and pour over cucumber and melon. Add parsley and toss gently. Add black pepper to taste and additional salt if needed. Sprinkle the salad with pistachios.

✣ Beet and Arugula Salad ✣
With Strawberries

By Chef Carl

INGREDIENTS

FOR THE DRESSING

- 1 tablespoon plus 2 teaspoons sherry vinegar
- 1 teaspoon balsamic vinegar
- Salt to taste
- ½ teaspoon Dijon mustard
- 4 tablespoons extra-virgin olive oil
- 1 tablespoon walnut oil

FOR THE SALAD

- 3 medium-size beets, roasted
- 1 bunch or 6-ounce bag arugula, preferably wild arugula (about 6 cups)
- ⅔ cup Strawberries
- 3 tablespoons broken walnuts

1-2 tablespoons chopped fresh tarragon

METHOD

- Whisk together vinegars, salt, Dijon mustard, olive oil and walnut oil.
- Peel beets and slice in half-moons or wedges. Place in a salad bowl and toss with 2 tablespoons of the dressing.
- Add remaining salad ingredients and remaining dressing, toss well and serve.

Roasted Sweet Potato and Kale Salad

By Chef Carl

INGREDIENTS

- 4 large unpeeled Sweet Potatoes, cut into 1/2-in.-thick wedges
- 2 tablespoons extra-virgin olive oil, divided
- 2 teaspoons coarsely ground coriander seeds
- 1/2 teaspoon black pepper
- 1/2 teaspoon salt, divided
- 6 tablespoons dried cranberries
- 6 tablespoons red wine vinegar
- 1 1/2 tablespoons brown sugar
- 2 teaspoons mustard seeds
- 1/2 small red onion, thinly vertically sliced
- 2 tablespoons fresh lemon juice
- 1 (7 1/2-oz.) bunch kale, stemmed and cut into 3/4-in.-wide strips

METHOD

- Preheat oven to 375°F.
- Combine Sweet Potatoes, 1 tablespoon olive oil, coriander seeds, pepper, and 1/4 teaspoon salt in a large bowl, tossing gently with hands to coat. Spread in a single layer on a baking sheet. Cover with foil. Bake at 375°F for 10 minutes. Remove foil; bake 15 more minutes or until Sweet Potato is tender and browned, turning once.
- While Sweet Potato roasts, combine cranberries, vinegar, brown sugar, mustard seeds, and 1/8 teaspoon salt in a small skillet over medium-low heat. Bring to a simmer; remove from heat. Steep 15 minutes or until almost all of the liquid is absorbed.
- Place onion in a bowl of ice-cold water; let stand 10 minutes. Drain

COOKING UP A CONVERSATION

- Toss lemon juice, kale, remaining 1 tablespoon olive oil, and remaining 1/8 teaspoon salt in a large bowl, massaging kale with hands to soften. Transfer kale to a large serving platter; top with Sweet Potato and onion. Sprinkle with cranberries.

Kale and Apple Salad

By Chef Carl

INGREDIENTS

- 3 tablespoons fresh lemon juice
- 2 tablespoons extra-virgin olive oil
- Sea salt
- 1 bunch kale, ribs removed, leaves very thinly sliced
- 1/4 cup dates
- 1 Gala Apple
- 1/4 cup slivered almonds, toasted
- 1-ounce Pecorino Cheese, finely grated (1/4 cup)
- Freshly ground black pepper

Method

- Whisk together the lemon juice, olive oil and 1/4 teaspoon salt in a large bowl. Add the kale, toss to coat and let stand 10 minutes.
- While the kale stands, cut the dates into thin slivers and the apple into thin matchsticks. Add the dates, apples, almonds and cheese to the kale. Season with salt and pepper and toss well.

Fruit Salad

By Chef Carl

INGREDIENTS

- 1 large mango, peeled and diced
- 2 cups fresh blueberries
- 2 bananas, sliced
- 2 cups fresh strawberries, halved
- 2 cups seedless grapes
- 2 nectarines, unpeeled and sliced
- 1 kiwi fruit, peeled and sliced

Honey orange sauce

- 1/3 cup unsweetened orange juice
- 2 tablespoons lemon juice
- 1 1/2 tablespoons honey
- 1/4 teaspoon ground ginger
- 1 dash nutmeg

METHOD

- Prepare the fruit.
- Combine all the ingredients for sauce and mix.
- Just before serving, pour honey orange sauce over the fruit, serve.

ENDIVE AND APPLE SALAD

By Chef Carl

INGREDIENTS

1/4 cup apple cider vinegar

1 teaspoon Dijon mustard

1 teaspoon minced shallot

1 teaspoon sugar

3/4 cup canola oil

3 heads of Belgian endive, halved lengthwise, cut crosswise into 1/2-inch pieces

1 cup torn escarole leaves

1/2 medium Gala apple, cored, cut into 6 wedges, thinly sliced crosswise

METHOD

Whisk first 4 ingredients in small bowl.

Gradually whisk in oil.

Season to taste with salt and pepper.

Set vinaigrette aside.

Mix Belgian endive, escarole, and apple in large bowl.

Toss salad with 1/4 cup vinaigrette.

RUBY- RED TURKEY SALAD
By Chef Dana

INGREDIENT

2 pounds smoked turkey breast
1 1/2 cup thinly sliced celery
1 1/4 cup dried tart cherries (Ruby)
1 cup walnuts, toasted and chopped
1/2 thinly sliced green onions
1 tablespoon of chopped fresh parsley
3/4 cup light mayonnaise
3/4 cup light sour cream
4 ounces Gorgonzola cheese, crumble
1/2 teaspoon salt
1 teaspoon fresh ground pepper

METHOD

In a large bowl, combine the turkey, celery, cherry, walnuts, green onions and parsley and toss well. In a separate bowl, whisk together the mayonnaise, sour cream, Gorgonzola, salt and pepper. Pour the dressing over the salad and toss well to coat thoroughly. Taste and adjust seasoning as needed and refrigerate

Cold Pasta Salad
By Chef Dana

INGREDIENTS

Extra virgin olive oil
2 bone-in skinless chicken breasts
Kosher salt and freshly ground pepper
1 pound plums, halved and pitted
1 pound penne pasta

Vinaigrette Dressing
1 tablespoon Dijon mustard
1 teaspoon red wine vinegar
1 teaspoon sugar
1/2 cup extra virgin olive oil
1 bunch fresh chives, minced
1 bunch parsley leaves, chopped
1/4-pound blue cheese, crumbled.
1/2 cup basil leaves

METHOD

Preheat the oven to 375. Place a cast iron skillet in over medium heat. Pour enough oil to coat bottom of pan, then heat till almost smoking. Sprinkle chicken breast with generous salt and pepper. Then place them in the pan. Cook for 5 minutes, until brown. Flip breast again then place in the oven for 15 minutes. When halfway done carefully take pan out and add plums halves cut side down. Put pan back in the oven a cook for 15 minutes. Until the chicken juices are clear and the plums are soft and juicy. Take the chicken and plums out if the pan and put in the refrigerator to chill.

Bring a big pot of salted water to a boil over high heat. Add the penne and give it a stir to keep the pasta from sticking together. Boil for 8 to 9 minutes or until al dente. Drain and chill.

To prepare the vinaigrette

whisk together the mustard, vinegar and sugar in a large serving bowl. Whisk in the oil and season with salt and pepper. Fold in the chives parsley.

Remove the chilled chicken from the bone and slice. Slice the plums. Toss the chicken and plums in the dressing. Toss the chilled pasta, blue cheese, and basil leaves and taste for seasoning.

 Shrimp Salad Sandwich

By Chef Dana

INGREDIENTS

1 pound cooked shrimp, chopped
1 cup finely diced celery
2 green onion thinly sliced
1/2 cup mayonnaise, plus more for spread
1/2 cup honey mustard
1 teaspoon freshly squeezed lemon juice
1 teaspoon salt
1/2 teaspoon freshly ground black pepper
8 slices cheddar cheese bread
4 leaves green leaf lettuce

METHOD

Combine the shrimp, celery, green onion, mayonnaise, mustard, lemon juice, salt and pepper in a large bowl and mix well. Taste and adjust the seasoning as necessary. Refrigerate for 1 day.

Toast the bread slices. Arrange a lettuce leaf on each bread slice. Top each lettuce with one quarter of the shrimp salad.

✤ Carolina Chopped Salad ✤

By Chef Dana

INGREDIENTS

White Balsamic Vinaigrette

1/2 cup white balsamic vinegar

1 egg

2 tablespoons minced shallots

2 tablespoons Dijon mustard

1 teaspoon salt

1 teaspoon freshly ground black pepper

1 cup olive oil

1 1/2 head romaine lettuce, julienned (8 cup)

6-ounce hard salami, julienned (1 cup)

1 rotisserie chicken, shredded meat (3 cup)

1 cup julienned provolone

1 pint grape tomatoes, halves

1 (15- ounce) can chickpeas, drained & rinsed

1 bunch basil, thinly sliced

1/2 cup shaved Parmesan cheese.

1/2 teaspoon salt

1/2 teaspoon freshly ground black pepper

COOKING UP A CONVERSATION

METHOD

To Prepare the Vinaigrette: combine the vinegar, egg, shallots, Dijon mustard, sakt and pepper in a blender and process.

With blender running add oil slowly, steady stream ti make emulsion. Salt and pepper to taste. Refrigerate for two days.

In a large bowl, combine the lettuce, salami, chicken, provolone, tomatoes, chickpeas, basil and Parmesan and toss lightly. Pour 1/2 cup of the dressing over the salt and pepper. Toss well to coat, garnish with Parmesan and serve immediately.

❈ Mandarin Soul Chicken Salad ❈

By Chef Dana

This Asia-style salad is a keeper. Especially when you add the homemade crispy wonton strips. Chef Dana's Sesame Dressing really adds the necessary pop to this salad.

INGREDIENTS

Soul Chicken and Marinade:

1/2 cup soy sauce

1/4 cup freshly squeezed orange juice

2 green onions julienne sliced

1 clove garlic minced

1 pound skinless chicken breast

Baked Wontons:

5 wonton skins, cut into 1/4 inch strips

Sesame Dressing:

1/3 cup sugar

3 tablespoons apple cider vinegar

2 1/4 teaspoon onion juice (smashed onions)

1 teaspoon soy sauce

1/2 teaspoon dry mustard

1/2 cup olive oil

1 tablespoon sesame seeds (toasted)

Salad:

5 bacon strips (turkey or pork)

1cup snow peas

1/4 cup diced red peppers

1can (8 oz.) water chestnuts drained

1can (11oz.) mandarin oranges, drained

1/2 head romaine lettuce, sliced 2 1/2 cups

2 bundles fresh spinach, sliced 2 1/2 cups

1/4 cup sliced almonds, toasted

2 tablespoons of black sesame seeds (garnish)

METHOD

To Assemble Salad: combine baked (diced) chicken, bacon, snow peas, bell pepper, water chestnut, oranges, spinach and lettuce in a large bowl. Add the dressing and toss. Top with wontons, garnish with almonds and sesame seeds and serve,

CORNBREAD

🟎 CORN BREAD 🟎

By Chef Dana

INGREDIENTS

1 ½ cups sugar

1 ½ cups cornmeal

4 eggs

12 teaspoons vanilla

½ cups milk

2 sticks butter

4 cups biscuit mix

METHOD

Preheat oven to 350°F. In a large bowl, cream sugar and butter. Add eggs and beat well. Add milk and vanilla and mix. Add cornmeal and biscuit mix, mixing until well blended. Grease and lightly flour 9x13- inch pan. Pour corn bread mixture into pan and bake for 30-35 mins.

COOKING UP A CONVERSATION

❈ LOW-FAT CORNBREAD ❈

By Chef Dana

Ingredients

1 cup yellow cornmeal

1 egg white

1 cup flour

1/8 teaspoon salt

¼ cup Splenda

1 cup skim milk

¼ cup egg substitute

2 tablespoons low-fat margarine

METHOD

Preheat oven to 350°F. In medium size bowl, mix all ingredients. Grease 9-inch square pan with non-stick spray and pour cornbread mixture into pan. Bake for about 25 minutes, or until top is brown.

✤ EASY CORNBREAD MUFFINS ✤

By Chef Dana

INGREDIENTS

1 (8 ½ ounce) box cornbread mix

1 stick butter or margarine, melted

1 ½ cups self-rising flour

1 ½ cups milk

3 eggs

¾ cup sugar

METHOD

Preheat oven to 350°F. In medium size bowl, combine all ingredients, stirring until well blended. Grease muffin tin with vegetable spray. Bake 20-25 minutes. Yield: 12 large muffins.

ENTREES

Chef Carl's
Healthy Fried n Baked Chicken

By Chef Carl

INGREDIENTS

2 chickens, frying size, cut up in pieces
2 tbsp. olive oil
2 onions, chopped
1 clove garlic, pressed
3 tsp. curry powder
1/2 tsp. dried thyme
1/2 c. toasted almonds
2 green bell peppers, sliced
1 1/2 tsp. salt
1/2 tsp. pepper
1 c. flour, as necessary
1/2 tsp. parsley flakes
5 c. canned tomatoes
3 tbsp. currants

METHOD

Wash and dry cut each chicken into 8 pieces. Salt, pepper and flour chicken. Fry in olive oil. Remove chicken and place in baking pan. Saute onions and garlic. Add tomatoes, almonds, currants and seasonings. Pour over chicken. Bake 45 minutes at 350 degrees. Serve over rice.

Sauteed Skate with Mushroom Veloute Sauce

By Chef Carl

1. For mushroom sauce

1 small leek, chopped

1 tablespoon olive oil

1 medium carrot, chopped

1/2 medium onion, chopped

1 garlic clove

1/4 cup dry white wine

2 cups water

1 teaspoon soy sauce

1 fresh flat-leaf parsley sprig

1 fresh thyme sprig

1 bay leaf

1 tablespoon crumbled dried porcini*

1 tablespoon quick-cooking tapioca

2. For sautéed mushrooms

1/2 tablespoon unsalted butter

1/2 tablespoon olive oil

6 oz mixed fresh mushrooms, such as oyster and chanterelle, trimmed and halved lengthwise or quartered if large

1/4 teaspoon salt

1/8 teaspoon black pepper

1 celery rib, thinly sliced diagonally

3. For skate

1 1/2 tablespoons all-purpose flour

1/4 teaspoon curry powder

2 (5- to 6-oz) pieces skate fillet, halved crosswise if large

1/2 teaspoon salt

1/8 teaspoon black pepper

1 1/2 tablespoons unsalted butter

METHOD

Make broth:

1. Wash chopped leek well in a bowl of cold water, agitating it, then lift out and pat dry.

2. Heat oil in a 3- to 4-quart heavy saucepan over moderately high heat until hot but not smoking, then sauté leek, carrot, onion, and garlic clove, stirring frequently, until vegetables are soft and well browned, about 10 minutes. Stir in wine and deglaze saucepan by boiling, stirring and scraping up any brown bits, 1 minute.

3. Add water, soy sauce, parsley, thyme, bay leaf, and porcini and simmer, uncovered, until liquid is reduced to 3/4 cup, about 25 minutes. Pour through a fine-mesh sieve into a glass measure, lightly pressing on and then discarding solids. Transfer to a small saucepan. If you have more than 3/4 cup, boil strained liquid a few minutes to reduce.

Sauté fresh mushrooms:

1. Heat butter and oil in a 10-inch heavy skillet until hot but not smoking, then sauté mushrooms with salt and pepper, stirring, until just tender and golden brown, about 4 minutes. Add celery and sauté until bright green and crisp-tender, about 2 minutes. Remove from heat and keep warm, covered with foil.

Finish sauce and sauté skate:

1. Bring broth to a simmer, then remove from heat and stir in tapioca. Let stand, covered, 10 to 15 minutes.

2. While sauce is standing, stir together flour and curry powder in a shallow bowl. Pat fish dry and sprinkle with salt and pepper, then dredge in flour mixture, shaking off excess and transferring to a plate as dredged.

3. Heat butter in a 12-inch heavy skillet over moderately high heat until foam subsides, then sauté fish, turning over once, until golden brown and just cooked through, about 5 minutes total.

4. Reheat sauce, then season with salt and pepper. Serve fish with sautéed mushrooms and sauce.

Baked Chicken Parmigiana

By Chef Carl

INGREDIENTS

2 large eggs

1 1/2 cups breadcrumbs or panko (Japanese breadcrumbs)

3/4 cup finely grated Parmesan (about 2 ounces)

5 tablespoons olive oil, divided, plus more for brushing

3 1/2 teaspoons dried oregano, divided

3/4 teaspoon kosher salt, divided

3/4 teaspoon freshly ground black pepper, divided

4 (6-ounce) chicken cutlets, pounded 1/2" thick

6 ounces coarsely grated mozzarella (about 1 cup)

1/2 medium onion, chopped

2 garlic cloves, pressed or finely chopped

1 (24-ounce) jar marinara sauce

1/4 teaspoon crushed red pepper flakes (optional)

1/4 cup (packed) basil leaves, torn if large, plus more for serving

METHOD

1. Arrange racks in top and bottom of oven and place a rimmed baking sheet on bottom rack; preheat to 450°F.
2. Beat eggs in a large shallow bowl. Using a fork or your fingertips, mix breadcrumbs, Parmesan, 3 Tbsp. oil, 3 tsp. oregano, 1/2 tsp. salt, and 1/2 tsp. pepper in another large shallow bowl or plate.
3. Working with 1 cutlet at a time, dip in egg, allowing excess to drip back into bowl. Dredge in breadcrumb mixture, shaking off excess, then pressing to adhere. Transfer chicken to a baking sheet.

4. Carefully remove preheated baking sheet from oven and generously brush with oil. Transfer chicken to baking sheet and return to bottom rack. Roast 6 minutes, then carefully flip (use a spatula to scrape under cutlets) and sprinkle with mozzarella. Place baking sheet on top rack and continue to roast until juices run clear, mozzarella is melted, and an instant-read thermometer inserted into the center of cutlet registers 165°F, about 4 minutes more.

5. Meanwhile, heat remaining 2 Tbsp. oil in a large skillet over medium-high. Cook onion, stirring, until softened, 3–4 minutes. Add garlic and cook until fragrant, about 1 minute more. Add marinara sauce, red pepper flakes (if using), 1/4 cup basil, and remaining 1/2 tsp. oregano, 1/4 tsp. salt, and 1/4 tsp. pepper. Cook, stirring, until sauce starts to bubble. Reduce heat to medium and simmer until chicken is ready, stirring occasionally, at least 5 minutes.

Divide sauce among 4 plates. Top with chicken and torn basil

Rock Shrimp n Grits

By Chef Carl

INGREDIENTS

water   3 ½ cups

stone ground grits   ¾ cup

Salt n White Pepper   to taste

rock shrimp in the shell   1 pound fresh

Hot Sauce   12 drops

Cheddar cheese, finely grated sharp   6 ounces

butter   3 tablespoons

peanut oil   ¼ cup

finely chopped scallions   1 cup

mushrooms, thinly sliced   6 ounces

garlic, finely minced   1 clove

Juice of 1 lemon

finely chopped parsley   ¼ cup

METHOD

1. Bring the water to boil and gradually add the grits, stirring. Add salt. Cook uncovered, stirring often, about 15 minutes. Cover closely and continue cooking over low heat for 25 minutes or until done.
2. Meanwhile, shell and devein shrimp and put in a bowl. Set aside.
3. When grits are cooked, remove from heat. Stir in 6 drops of Tabasco sauce, the cheese and butter.
4. Place two heavy skillets on the stove. Add the diced bacon to one skillet; pour the oil in the other. Cook the bacon, stirring, until it starts to brown. Add the shrimp and cook, tossing and stirring so that they cook evenly, about 3 minutes. Add scallions and cook briefly.
5. As the shrimp cook, put the mushrooms in the hot oil in the other skillet and cook, tossing and stirring, until the mushrooms give up their liquid. Add the garlic and cook briefly, stirring. Add the lemon juice and stir.
6. Combine the shrimp and mushroom mixtures in one skillet and sprinkle with parsley and the remaining Tabasco. Stir to blend.
7. Spoon equal portions of the cheese grits onto six hot plates. Spoon equal portions of the shrimp and mushroom mixture over each serving. Serve immediately.

Shrimp n Quinoa Burgers

By Chef Carl

INGREDIENTS

Shrimp, medium   *1 pound*
scallions, chopped   *2 tablespoons*
celery, diced   *3 tablespoons*
parsley, chopped   *2 tablespoons*
lemon zest   *1 ½ teaspoons*
mayonnaise   *3 tablespoons*
bread crumbs   *1 cup*
egg, beaten   *1*
Salt and pepper   *to taste*
Tabasco sauce   *to taste*
peanut oil   *1 tablespoon*
Quinoa, cooked   *1 Cup*

PREPARATION

1. Boil shrimp for 2 minutes. Drain in a colander, and place ice on top until cool enough to handle. Peel and devein shrimp, and chop into small dice.
2. In a large bowl, mix shrimp with quinoa, scallions, celery, parsley and lemon zest. Stir in mayonnaise, cornbread crumbs and the egg, and beat with a whisk or wooden spoon until evenly distributed. Season with salt, pepper and Tabasco to taste.
3. With your hands, form 6 patties about 3 inches in diameter. Sauté, 3 at a time, in peanut oil until both sides are nicely browned. Drain on paper towels. Serve on hamburger buns with lettuce, tomato and tartar sauce.

COOKING UP A CONVERSATION

Herbed Roast Chicken With Lemon

By Chef Carl

INGREDIENTS

1 chicken   *2 1/2 to 3 1/2 pounds*

medium-grained sea salt   *½ Cup*

mixed herbs *(sage, thyme, rosemary, oregano)*, coarsely chopped   *1 ounce fresh*

lemons, large   *2*

Olive oil   *½ Cup*

Carrots, onions, leeks, turnips or other vegetables for roasting, as desired

chicken stock   *½ cup*

PREPARATION

1. Working carefully to prevent tearing, loosen the skin over as much of the chicken as possible by slipping your hand under it. Rub the chicken flesh lightly with salt, and slide the herbs under the skin. (You should be able to see them through the skin.)
2. Place all the lemon in the chicken's cavity, and cover the chicken in plastic wrap or foil. Refrigerate overnight.
3. Heat oven to 400 degrees. Lightly coat the bottom of a roasting pan with olive oil. Unwrap the chicken and place it breast side up in the pan, surrounded by any vegetables to be roasted. Drizzle the vegetables with oil, turning them to coat well. Roast for 20 minutes, then baste the chicken and vegetables with pan juices. If there are no juices, add 1/4 cup water to the pan, scraping the bottom, and baste.
4. Reduce temperature to 325 degrees. Continue basting every 10 to 15 minutes until the juices run clear when the chicken is pierced at the thigh, about 20 minutes to a pound. Roast vegetables until browned and caramelized, removing when cooked to taste. Transfer the chicken to a platter and keep warm. Remove the lemon from the cavity and place in the roasting pan, mashing it a bit to release the juices. Place pan on low heat and add the chicken stock, scraping the bottom of the pan. Carve the chicken, adding any juices to the pan. Pour the hot juices into a pitcher or gravy boat. Serve the chicken and vegetables, passing the juices separately.

COOKING UP A CONVERSATION

✿ Sweet Bourbon-Glazed Salmon ✿

By Chef Carl

INGREDIENTS

brown sugar   *1 cup packed*

bourbon   *6 tablespoons*

soy sauce low-sodium   *1/4 cup*

fresh lime juice   *2 tablespoons*

fresh ginger, grated peeled   *2 teaspoons*

salt   *1/2 teaspoon*

black pepper, ground   *1/4 teaspoon*

garlic cloves, crushed   *2*

salmon fillets   *6-ounce*

Cooking spray

sesame seeds   *4 teaspoons*

Scallions, thinly sliced   *1/2 cup*

METHOD

* Combine the first 8 ingredients in a large zip-top freezer bag; add salmon fillets. Seal freezer bag, and marinate in refrigerator 30 minutes, turning bag once. Remove fillets from bag; discard marinade.
* Preheat broiler.
* Place fillets on broiler pan coated with cooking spray. Broil 11 minutes or until fish flakes easily when tested with a fork. Sprinkle each fillet with 1/2 teaspoon sesame seeds and 1 tablespoon onions.

❈ Seared Scallops with Arugula and ❈ Great Northern White Beans

By Chef Carl

INGREDIENTS

olive oil   *2 tablespoons*

sea scallops   *1 1/2 pounds*

salt   *1/4 teaspoon*

onion, diced   *1 cup*

red pepper, crushed   *1/8 teaspoon*

garlic cloves, minced   *2*

white wine, dry   *1/4 cup*

chicken broth fat-free, less-sodium   *1 cup*

Northern white beans, rinsed and drained   *1 (19-ounce) can*

Arugula, fresh   *1 (6-ounce) package*

Basil, fresh chopped   *2 tablespoons*

METHOD

* Heat 1 tablespoon oil in a large nonstick skillet over medium-high heat. Sprinkle scallops evenly with salt. Add scallops to pan; cook 2 minutes on each side or until done. Remove scallops from pan; keep warm.
* Add remaining 1 tablespoon oil and onion to pan; sauté 2 minutes. Add pepper and garlic; cook 20 seconds, stirring constantly. Stir in wine; cook 1 minute or until most of liquid evaporates.
* Stir in broth and beans; cook 2 minutes
* Add arugula cook 1 minute or until arugula wilts
* Remove from heat; stir in basil

Crab Cakes with Spicy Rémoulade

By Chef Carl

INGREDIENTS

Crab cakes:

jumbo lump crabmeat   *1 pound*
onion finely chopped   *2 tablespoons*
canola mayonnaise   *1 1/2 tablespoons*
black pepper   *1/4 teaspoon*
parsley, finely chopped   *2*
egg, large lightly beaten   *1*
panko bread crumbs, divided   *1 cup*
canola oil, divided   *2 tablespoons*

Remoulade:

canola mayonnaise   *1/4 cup*
shallots, minced   *2 teaspoons*
parsley chopped fresh   *1 teaspoon*
Dijon mustard   *1 1/2 teaspoons*
cayenne pepper, ground   *1 teaspoon*

METHOD

To prepare crab cakes, drain crabmeat on several layers of paper towels. Combine crabmeat, bell pepper, and the next 4 ingredients (through egg), tossing gently. Stir in 1/4 cup panko. Place remaining 3/4 cup panko in a shallow dish.

Divide crab mixture into 8 equal portions. Shape 4 portions into 3/4-inch-thick patties; dredge in panko. Heat a large nonstick skillet over medium-high heat. Add 1 tablespoon oil. Add dredged patties; cook 3 minutes on each side or until golden. Remove from pan. Repeat procedure with the remaining crab mixture, panko, and oil.

To prepare rémoulade, combine 1/4 cup mayonnaise and remaining ingredients; serve with crab cakes

Quick Jerk-Rubbed Red Snapper with Spicy Cilantro Slaw

By Chef Carl

INGREDIENTS

3 cups cabbage-and-carrot coleslaw mix

2 tablespoons chopped fresh cilantro

3 tablespoons canola mayonnaise

2 tablespoons fresh lime juice

1 1/2 teaspoons sugar

1 to 1 1/2 teaspoons finely chopped habanero

Cooking spray

4 (6-ounce) red snapper fillets

4 teaspoons Jamaican jerk seasoning

METHOD

Combine first 6 ingredients in a medium bowl; toss well to coat.
Heat a grill pan over medium-high heat. Coat pan with cooking spray. Sprinkle fish evenly with jerk seasoning. Add fish to pan; cook 3 minutes on each side or until desired degree of doneness. Remove from heat; serve fish with slaw.

Sweet Potato - Potato Salad

By Chef Carl

INGREDIENTS

Sweet Potatoes (cooked until tender and then cubed and cooled)   *3 pounds*

Hard cooked eggs (cooled and coarsely chopped)   *5-6*

red onion, chopped   *1/4-1/2 cup*

celery, chopped   *1/4-1/2 cup*

sweet relish   *1/2 cup*

Mayonnaise   *3/4 cup*

yellow mustard   *1-2 tablespoons*

salt and pepper   *to taste*

thinly sliced tomatoes and cucumber for garnish

METHOD

Combine sweet potatoes or yams, egg, onions, and celery. Stir in sweet relish, mayonnaise, mustard, and salt and pepper to taste. (Stir the mayonnaise and mustard in a little at a time, until you have the flavor and consistency you like.)
Top with thinly sliced tomatoes and cucumber, if desired.

Gouda n Broccoli Stuffed Chicken

By Chef Carl

INGREDIENTS

Broccoli, fresh   *1 bunch*

smoked gouda cheese (thinly sliced)   *3 cups*

boneless chicken breasts   *6*

salt and pepper   *to taste*

paprika   *to taste*

BBQ sauce   *1 cup*

METHOD

Wash and chop broccoli into very small pieces.
Cut a "pocket" in each chicken breast by cutting lengthwise down one side of the breast (do not "butterfly" the chicken breast, it should only have a cut for the "pocket" down one side!).
Season each breast with salt, pepper, and paprika.
Stuff each "pocket" with broccoli and cheese. Use the toothpicks to wind through and sew the pocket shut.
Place the chicken on the grill to produce hash marks on the chicken breasts.
Finish in a 350°F oven for 15 minutes or until and heat until thoroughly cooked.
Plate each breast with 1 tablespoon of BBQ sauce on bottom.

❈ Braised Chicken ❈ With Lemon and Olives

By Chef Carl

INGREDIENTS

chicken thighs, skin-on and bone-in   *8*

Salt and pepper   *to taste*

crushed red pepper flakes   *½ teaspoon*

garlic cloves, minced   *4*

rosemary, fresh, roughly chopped   *1 tablespoon*

olive oil   *1 tablespoon*

lemons, cut in wedges   *2*

olives with pits, a mixture of black and green   *1 cup*

chicken broth   *1 cup*

chopped parsley   *3 tablespoons*

METHOD

Pat chicken thighs dry with paper towels. Season well with salt and pepper and place in an earthenware baking dish in one layer, skin side up. Sprinkle with red pepper, garlic, fennel and rosemary and drizzle with olive oil. Rub seasoning into thighs on all sides. Tuck lemon wedges here and there. Let marinate for 15 minutes. Heat oven to 375 degrees.

Put baking dish in oven, uncovered, and roast until skin browns lightly, about 20 minutes. Scatter olives evenly over chicken and add broth. Cover tightly and bake for 1 hour, until meat is very tender when probed with a skewer.

Remove thighs and lemon wedges and arrange on a platter. Keep warm. Pour pan juices into a saucepan and quickly skim fat from surface. Over high heat, simmer rapidly until reduced by half. Spoon juices over chicken, sprinkle with parsley and serve

✖ Asian Spiced Rubbed Chicken ✖

By Chef Dana

INGREDIENTS

40 Chicken pieces or

20 Whole Chicken Wings

Tablespoon Cayenne Pepper

2 Chinese 5-spice Powder

Kosher Salt and Pepper To Taste

Yield: 40 wings

Cilantro Dipping Sauce

1/3 cup chopped fresh cilantro

1/4 cup light sour cream

1/4 cup light mayonnaise

1/4 plain yogurt

1/2 whole lemon (juice)

Yield: 1 cup

COOKING UP A CONVERSATION

METHOD

Preheat oven to 500 degrees. If you have whole Chicken wings, cut off the tips and cut wings in half at the joint. Place wings in a large bowl. Sprinkle five spice powder and cayenne pepper on the wings. Add generous pinches of salt and 17 grinds of black pepper. Rub the mixture into all the wings until no more loose rub remains.

Line the wing pieces up on a baking sheet so the wing that has the most skin is facing up. Roast until cooked through, browned and crispy, about 25 minutes. Served with the cilantro dipping sauce.

Cilantro Dipping Sauce:

Combine all ingredients through the lemon juice in a mixing bowl. Whisk incorporate fully and season with salt and black pepper to taste.

✤ Spaghetti w/ Asparagus ✤
Smoked Mozzarella & Prosciutto

By Chef Dana

INGREDIENTS

2-pound asparagus, trimmed

3/4-pound spaghetti

4 tablespoon olive oil

4 garlic cloves, minced

6 ounces thinly sliced prosciutto

6 ounces smoked mozzarella (diced)

6 tablespoons thinly sliced fresh basil.

Yields: 6 to 8 servings

METHOD

Cook the asparagus in large pot of boiling salted water until crisp-tender, about 3 minutes. Remove the asparagus from the water to a bowl of ice to cool and stop cooking.

Boil water and add the paste and cook till al dente, tender but still a firm bite. About 8 minutes. Drain and set aside.

Heat the oil in a large skillet over medium heat. Add the garlic and sauté until fragrant. Add the asparagus to the skillet and season with salt and black pepper to taste. Add paste. Toss olive oil to coat. Add prosciutto and mozzarella and basil and toss to combine. Turn off heat. Season salt and pepper to taste.

Knowledge: Prosciutto is Italian for Ham. It the salt cured rear leg of a pig. Look for Prosciutto di Parma for real flavor.

Cooking the asparagus this way by cooling with ice water is called blanching. It works great for vegetables. Keeps them bright and crisp.

Seared Pork Tenderloin w/ Cocoa-Spice Rub

By Chef Dana

INGREDIENTS

1 tablespoon whole white peppercorn

1 tablespoon whole coriander seeds

4 tablespoons ground cinnamon

2 tablespoon ground nutmeg

1 tablespoon ground cloves

1 tablespoon minced garlic

3 1/2 tablespoons unsweetened coco

4 tablespoon sea salt

2 12 to 16- ounces pork tenderloin

2 tablespoons extra-virgin olive oil

Yields: 4 servings

METHOD

Preheat the oven to 400 degrees. In a medium saucepan over medium heat, toast white peppercorn and coriander seeds until they began to pop. Remove from heat and grind to a fine powder. Mix the garlic ground pepper and remaining spices coco and salt.

Trim the pork tenderloin of fat and sliver skin. Rub with a generous amount of coco spice rub. Heat olive oil in a large skillet over medium heat until hot but not smoking.

Sear each tenderloin on all sides until it a rich brown color, about 2 minutes on each side. Remove tenderloin from heat, place in oven and roast until 155 degrees. (about 12 to 15 minutes)

Let the tenderloin rest out of the oven for 10 minutes before carving.

COOKING UP A CONVERSATION

Baby Back Ribs w/ Georgia Peach BBQ Sauce

By Chef Dana

INGREDIENTS

2 rack baby back ribs(4 to 6 ribs per person)

Sea Salt and freshly ground pepper

Georgia Peach BBQ Sauce

4 tablespoon olive oil

4 tablespoon minced garlic

1 cup apple cider vinegar

1/2 cup soy sauce

2 cups ketchup

2 cups honey

2 8 ounces can of peaches

sea salt and pepper to taste

Yields: 5 to 6 cups

METHOD

Preheat oven to 325 degrees. Cut each rack of ribs in half along the bone so they can easily be stacked.

Sprinkle liberally with salt and black pepper. On both sides pat into meat. (make sure to over season the ribs inevitably come off in the pan).

On a cookie sheet lined with aluminum foil. Shingle the ribs close together. Put in oven, rotating the layers every 30 minutes. Until they are tender. Almost falling of the bone. About 2 hours.

Half an hour before serving. Transfer ribs to pre heated grill on low heat. Brush ribs with BBQ sauce. Close the grill. Grill the ribs turning and brush with sauce every 10 minutes until rib are well glazed (About 30 minutes)

Shrimp Ceviche
w/ Melon, Chile and Mint

By Chef Dana

INGREDIENTS

2 pounds of shrimp

Sea Salt and freshly ground pepper to taste.

2 tablespoons garlic

3 tablespoon seafood seasoning

juice of 3 oranges

juice of 3 lemon

juice of 3 limes

zest of 1 oranges

zest of 1 lemon

zest of 1 lime

2 teaspoons granulated sugar

1/4 cup olive oil

Cantaloupe salad

1 small cantaloupe halved, seeded and peeled and cut into small cubes

1/2 bunch fresh mint leaves, hand torn.

1 fresh red Chile, paper thin circle

Yields: 12 servings

METHOD

Make the ceviche put shrimp in a glass bowl and adds a fair amount of salt and pepper to taste and garlic and seafood seasoning.

Cook on low heat for about 2 to 3 minutes.

Put the juices and zest and sugar in a blender and give them the whirl to combine. Add olive oil and blend again to emulsify. Pour the marinade over shrimp there should be enough juice to allow the shrimp to float freely. Cover and refrigerate for 2 and a half hours. Until the shrimp are opaque.

Make the cantaloupe salad in a separate bowl combine the cantaloupe mint, and chili, salt and pepper to taste and toss gently to combine.

Add salad on top of ceviche

COOKING UP A CONVERSATION

FAMILY REUNION SPAGHETTI

BY CHEF DANA

INGREDIENTS

4 Pounds lean ground beef

1 cup water

Salt and black pepper, to taste

4 tablespoons grated Parmesan cheese

6 pounds mild Italian sausage

4 tablespoons freshly ground anise seeds

3 tablespoons olive oil

1 large can pitted black olives, sliced

2 cups chopped red onions

4 large packages pasta

5 ribs celery, chopped

Salt, to taste

4 red bell peppers, chopped

Butter or olive oil

3 tablespoons minced garlic

3 (14 ½ ounce) cans diced tomatoes

5 jars prepared tomato sauce

 (preferred brand containing Merlot)

METHOD

In large saucepan, cook ground beef over medium heat, stirring to beak meat into small pieces. Remove meat, drain, season and set aside in large mixing bowl. Place sausage into same saucepan and cook over medium heat, covered, about 30 minutes. Remove, drain, slice into bite size pieces and add to ground beef. In original large saucepan, sauté onions in olive oil, adding small amounts of water to soften.

Cook until transparent. Add celery; sauté. Add bell peppers; sauté. Add garlic and diced tomatoes and sauté for a short time. Into a very large cooking pot, place reserved meats, add sautéed vegetables and tomato sauce. Use water to rinse jars and add to pot. Continue cooking on medium heat. Add Parmesan cheese, anise, olives and seasoning. Cover and simmer 30 minutes.

In very large pot, prepare pasta according to package directions. Remove, rinse, drain and add butter or olive oil to keep pasta separated. Serve sauce over pasta along with French bread. Yield: 30 servings.

For large portions such as this, try cooking pasta in small, separate portions. This meal can be ready in 3 hours. Sauce can be made ahead of time and refrigerated.

Fingerling Potatoes w/sage blue cheese and bacon

(Upscale Potato skins)

By Chef Dana

INGREDIENTS

1-pound fingerling potatoes

2 tablespoons extra virgin olive oil

Sea Salt and freshly ground pepper

4 slices smoked bacon

12 sage leaves

1/3 cup crumble blue cheese

1/2 cup lite ranch dressing (dipping)

METHOD

Preheat oven to 400 F. In a bowl, toss the potatoes with oil and salt to taste. Spread evenly over a baking sheet. Roast for 20 minutes. Allow to cool. Slice the potatoes in half. Pour remaining oil into a sauté pan. Place over medium heat and add sage to sauté for a minute. Transfer to a paper towel.

Place bacon on a baking sheet, cook for 12 minutes, remove a place on a paper towel. Chop the bacon. Place potatoes cut side up in a baking dish, sprinkle on the bacon and then the blue cheese. Place in the oven for 4 minutes or until cheese soften. Then garnish with sage leaves

FRESH ORANGE CHICKEN

By Chef Dana

INGREDIENTS

2 broiler-fryers (3 pounds each)   cut into serving pieces

½ cup dry white wine OR   canned chicken consommé

Salt and pepper

2 tablespoons sugar

1 cup chopped onion

2 tablespoons freshly squeezed lemon juice

 1 cup chopped onion

2 tablespoons grated orange peel

3 oranges, peeled and sliced into cartwheels

METHOD

Season chicken well with salt and pepper. Sauté in butter over medium heat until golden brown on all sides. Add onions; sauté until soft. Transfer to shallow baking pan;

cover with mixture of orange peel, orange juice and wine. Bake uncovered at 375° for 45 minutes or until tender, turning during baking.

Place chicken on serving platter; keep warm. Strain pan drippings; reserve. In small saucepan, melt sugar over medium, heat just until golden. Remove from heat; immediately stir in lemon juice, then drippings. Bring to a boil, stirring until caramel is melted. Briskly simmer 7-10 minutes until slightly syrupy. Add orange cartwheels; heat until warm. Pour over chicken; serve at once. Yield: 8-10 servings.

✥ LOW-FAT CHICKEN GUMBO ✥

(For a party over 30 people)

By Chef Dana

INGREDIENTS

50-pound chicken, uncooked

48 ounces' chicken broth

15 pounds smoked sausage, cut into Small chunks

3 gallons' oyster juice (approximate)

5 pounds' dry roux (browned flour)

Salt to taste, Pepper to taste

6 pounds' onions, chopped

6 bell peppers, chopped

½ gallon oysters (optional)

Gumbo filé, to taste

METHOD

The night before cooking the gumbo, pre-boil chicken and sausage. (I recommend Hillshire Farms Smoked Sausage.) De-bone chicken to make approximately 40 pounds of meat. After cooling, refrigerate chicken, sausage and chicken-sausage stock. The next day, skim and discard the jelled layer of fat on stock.

Into heavy 80-quart boiling pot, pour stock and enough water to fill pot more than half. Bring liquid to boil. Using 1 cup of roux at a time, whisk together with water, until well blended. Add to boiling stock and stir well.

Add onions, bell peppers, chicken broth, oyster juice, salt and pepper. Cook at low to boil for a few hours. Add chicken, sausage and oysters an hour before ready to serve.

Boil until oysters are cooked and chicken is tender but not falling apart. Sprinkle in filé, 1 tablespoon at a time, stirring after each addition, until gumbo reaches desired consistency. (4 tablespoons of file for this size gumbo is usually enough.) Turn off heat and let gumbo sit at least 1 hour before serving. Yield: 200-250 servings.

Pan-roasted Halibut w/ Prosciutto Lemon, White Wine Caper

By Chef Dana

INGREDIENTS

1/2 cup all-purpose flour

sea salt and pepper to taste

2 -6-ounce halibut filets

2 tablespoons olive oil

3 tablespoon butter

2 slices prosciutto, cut into strips

1/2 cup white wine

juice 1/2 lemon

2 tablespoons caper

2 tablespoons chopped fresh parsley

Yields: 2 servings

METHOD

Preheat oven to 375 degrees. Put the flour on a deep plate or in a shallow bowl and season well with salt and black pepper. Dredge the fish in the flour. Put a medium oven-safe skillet over medium heat, add tablespoon oil and 1 tablespoon butter, and get the skillet hot. Add the filet, skin side up, and cook until browned on one side. 2 to 3 minutes. At the same time add the prosciutto and cook, stirring to brown. Then flip the fish, put the skillet in the oven, and roast till the fish is cooked through, about 10 minutes.

Remove the fish. Drain the prosciutto on a paper towel. Put the skillet back over the medium heat. Add remaining oil and butter, white wine, lemon juice, capers and parsley and bring to a boil: keep at a boil until reduced and thickened. Season with salt and black pepper to taste. Pour the sauce over the fish, top with the prosciutto.

Apricot- Glazed Chicken w/ Dried Plum & Sage

By Chef Dana

INGREDIENTS

2 -4 to 5-pound roasting chickens, cut into pieces

1 -12-ounce jar apricot preserves

15 medium dried plums, pitted

1/3 cup olive oil

1 tablespoon white vinegar

1 tablespoon sea salt

1 tablespoon ground pepper

10 cloves of garlic, peeled

25 safe leaves

Yields: 8 servings

METHOD

Preheat the oven to 400 degrees. Trim any extra fat from the chicken pieces and transfer them to a foil lined sheet pan or broiler pan. Toss all the ingredients together with the chicken until the chicken is evenly coated with the sauce. Arrange the chicken pieces, skin side up, in the pan, spaced evenly apart.

Roast until the tops of the chicken pieces are browned and the chicken is cooked through, and the juices run clear. (About 35- 40 minutes) Or temperature of 165 degrees.

Stuffed Pork Chops w/ Grits

By Chef Dana

INGREDIENTS

Pork

4 -1 1/2 to 2-inch-thick pork chops Bone in, split to the bone

1-pound bulk sausage, split into 4 equal portions

1/4 cup sea salt

1/4 cup pepper

1/4 cup garlic powder

1/4 cup onion powder

olive oil, for brushing

Grits

2 cups water

1 1/4 cup milk

1 teaspoon salt

1 cup quick cook grits (not instant)

1/2 cup butter

METHOD

For the pork: Preheat grill. Stuff each pork chop with the sausage. Rub liberally with all ingredients. Secure each pork chop with a toothpick or a wooden skewer. (Remember to remove before serving). Brush oil on grill grate to prevent sticking. Grill the chops over direct heat till browned about 5 to 6 minutes on each side. Move off direct heat. Cook until pork, temp. using a thermometer till it reads 165 degrees.

For the grits: In a small pot, bring the water, milk and salt to a boil. Slowly stir the grits into the boiling mixture. Stir continuously and thoroughly until the grits are well mixed. Lower the heat and simmer for 4 minutes. Stir occasionally add more water if needed. Grits are done when they have the consistency of smooth cream. Then stir in half of the butter. Remaining butter divided equally.

Pesto-Stuffed Salmon with Tomato-Corn Salad

By Chef Dana

INGREDIENTS

SALMON

½ cup loosely packed fresh basil

½ cup loosely packed fresh parsley

2 tablespoons blanched whole almonds

¼ teaspoon minced garlic

¼ teaspoon kosher salt, plus additional for seasoning

Freshly ground black pepper

3 tablespoons extra-virgin olive oil, plus additional for brushing

1 ½-pound center-cut skinless Salmon fillet

Vegetable oil for grilling

SALAD

1 pound ripe mixed small tomatoes, halved or diced

1 cup cooked fresh corn kernels (from 2 ears)

3 tablespoons extra-virgin olive oil

1 tablespoon white wine vinegar

2 teaspoons minced fresh marjoram or oregano

Kosher salt and freshly ground black pepper

Yield: 4 servings

METHOD

For the salmon: Pulse the basil, parsley, almonds garlic, ¼ teaspoon salt, and black pepper to taste in a food processor to make a coarse paste. With the motor running, drizzle in the olive oil until incorporated. Next, cut the pocket. Hold the pocket open, season the inside with salt and black pepper to taste, and spread the pesto evenly inside the fish with a spoon. (The fish can be prepared up to this point a day ahead of grilling, then covered and refrigerated.)

Prepare an outdoor grill with a medium-high fire.

Lightly brush the grill grate with oil. Brush the fillet on both sides with the olive oil and season the flesh side with salt and black pepper to taste. Lay the fish, flesh side down, on the grill and cook until there are distinct grill marks and you can lift the fish without it sticking, about 3 to 5 minutes. (test it by gently lifting a corner- if it sticks, let it cook a bit longer.)

When it lifts cleanly, carefully turn it about 45 degrees from its original position (don't turn it over). Cook for another 3 minutes, until marked. Season the skin side with salt and black pepper to taste, turn the fillet over, and cook about 3 to 5 minutes more, or until the instant-read thermometer inserted in the side registers about 125°F.

Transfer the fish to a plate and let it rest for 5 minutes. Cut salmon into 4 equal pieces and transfer to serving plates. Serve salmon warm or at room temperature topped with the Tomato-Corn Salad. Drizzle with any extra juices from the salad.

For the salad: Toss the tomatoes with corn. Add the olive oil, vinegar, marjoram, and salt and black pepper to taste. Toss again taking care not to break up the tomatoes.

✥ SHRIMP AND EGGPLANT ✥ CASSEROLE

By Chef Dana

INGREDIENTS

4 medium eggplants

1 egg, beaten

1 medium onion, chopped

¼ cup grated Colby or Monterey Jack cheese

1 bell pepper, chopped

1 clove garlic, minced

¼ cup bread crumbs

1 tablespoon margarine

Salt

1 ½ cups peeled shrimp

Pepper

METHOD

Preheat oven to 350°F. Peel and cut eggplants and boil in salted water until soft. Drain and mash. Set aside. In saucepan, sauté onion, bell pepper and eggplant, add egg, cheese and sautéed vegetables. Stir well and pour into greased casserole dish.

Sprinkle with bread crumbs. Bake 45 minutes or until brown and bubbly.

1 cup crabmeat or 1 ½ cups crawfish may be substituted.

DESSERTS

✤ 4 Berries n Ginger Pie ✤

By Chef Carl

INGREDIENTS

- ⅔ cup granulated sugar
- 1 teaspoon lemon zest
- 5 tablespoons cornstarch
- 1 tablespoon very finely grated, peeled fresh ginger
- 4 cups blueberries
- 2 cups blackberries
- 2 cups raspberries
- 2 cups strawberries
- 1 tablespoon freshly squeezed lemon juice
- Pinch kosher salt

METHOD

In a large bowl, combine the sugar and lemon zest. Rub the zest into the sugar with your fingertips until well combined and fragrant. Stir in the cornstarch and fresh ginger. Add the blueberries, blackberries and raspberries and strawberries to the bowl. Sprinkle the lemon juice over the top, but don't stir quite yet. Let sit while you make the dough.

Place one disk of the pie dough on a lightly floured surface. With a lightly floured rolling pin, roll the dough into a 12-inch-wide circle 1/8 to 1/4 inch thick. Fit it into a 9-inch pie dish, trim any rough edges, leaving a 1-inch overhang, and set it in the fridge while you roll the other crust and cut the lattice.

Roll the second disk of pie dough into a circle roughly 12 inches wide and 1/8 to 1/4 inch thick. Use a pastry wheel or knife to cut the dough into strips about 1 1/2 inches wide.

Gently stir the filling together until well mixed and pour it into the pie dish. Press gently to pack down the berries into the dish.

Weave the dough strips into a lattice. Trim off any excess dough and fold the edges of the bottom crust up and over the lattice strips. Crimp together the edges. Slide the whole pie into the freezer until the crust is very firm, about 15 minutes. While the pie is chilling, heat the oven to 400 degrees and set a rack in the bottom third of the oven.

After the pie has chilled, place it on a baking sheet to catch any drips. Beat the egg, then brush the top of the pie with the egg wash and sprinkle with turbinado sugar and flaky salt.

Bake the pie until it is deep golden brown and the juices are bubbling, 45 to 55 minutes. If the crust begins to burn before the filling bubbles, tent it with aluminum foil. Cool before serving.

Fruit Cobbler

By Chef Dana

INGREDIENTS

1 ¾ cups all-purpose flour

¼ cup granulated sugar

1 tablespoon baking powder

½ teaspoon baking soda

⅛ teaspoon kosher salt

6 tablespoons cold unsalted butter, cubed

½ cup buttermilk

¼ cup plus 1 tablespoon heavy cream

10 cups mixed peaches and blueberries

2/3 cup granulated sugar, to taste

3 tablespoons minute tapioca

1 tablespoon turbinado

METHOD

Place a piece of parchment paper on a small rimmed baking sheet or large plate.

In a food processor, pulse together flour, granulated sugar, baking powder, baking soda and salt. Pulse in butter just until mixture looks like small pebbles. Drizzle in buttermilk and cream, and pulse just to combine.

Transfer to a lightly floured surface and pat dough together, incorporating any stray or dry pieces. Using a spoon, scoop off 2-inch pieces of dough and roll into balls (you should end up with about 10). Transfer dough to baking sheet or plate and flatten balls to 3/4-inch thick; wrap with plastic and chill for at least 20 minutes, and up to 8 hours.

Heat oven to 350 degrees. In a large bowl, toss together fruit, sugar to taste, and tapioca. Let sit for 20 minutes to hydrate tapioca, then scrape into a 2 1/2-quart gratin dish or 9-by-13-inch baking pan.

Top with biscuits, then brush biscuit tops with remaining 1 tablespoon cream. Sprinkle with turbinado sugar, and bake until dark golden on top and fruit is bubbling in the middle, about 1 hour, rotating halfway through. Let cool for at least 30 minutes before serving.

Banana Pudding

By Chef Carl

INGREDIENTS

2/3 cup white sugar

1/3 cup all-purpose flour

1/4 teaspoon salt

3 eggs, beaten

2 cups milk

1/2 teaspoon vanilla extract

2 tablespoons butter, softened

2 bananas, peeled and sliced

1/2 (12 ounce) package vanilla wafer cookies

METHOD

In medium saucepan combine sugar, flour, and salt. Add eggs and stir well. Stir in milk, and cook over low heat, stirring constantly. When mixture begins to thicken, remove from heat and continue to stir, cooling slightly. Stir in vanilla and butter until smooth.

Layer pudding with bananas and vanilla wafers in a serving dish. Chill at least one hour in refrigerator before serving.

Sweet Potato Pie

By Chef Carl

INGREDIENTS

1 (1 pound) sweet potato

1/2 cup butter, softened

1 cup white sugar

1/2 cup milk

2 eggs

1/2 teaspoon ground nutmeg

1/2 teaspoon ground cinnamon

1 teaspoon vanilla extract

1 (9 inch) unbaked pie crust

METHOD

Boil sweet potato whole in skin for 40 to 50 minutes, or until done. Run cold water over the sweet potato, and remove the skin.

Break apart sweet potato in a bowl. Add butter, and mix well with mixer. Stir in sugar, milk, eggs, nutmeg, cinnamon and vanilla. Beat on medium speed until mixture is smooth. Pour filling into an unbaked pie crust.

Bake at 350 degrees F (175 degrees C) for 55 to 60 minutes, or until knife inserted in center comes out clean. Pie will puff up like a soufflé, and then will sink down as it cools.

Red Velvet Cake

By Chef Carl

INGREDIENTS

1/2 cup shortening

1 1/2 cups white sugar

2 eggs, room temperature

1 teaspoon butter flavored extract

4 tablespoons red food coloring

2 tablespoons unsweetened cocoa powder

1 cup buttermilk, room temperature

1 teaspoon salt

2 1/2 cups sifted all-purpose flour

1 tablespoon white vinegar

1 teaspoon baking soda

Cream Cheese Frosting:

1/2 cup butter, room temperature

1 (8 ounce) package cream cheese, room temperature

4 cups confectioners' sugar, sifted

1 teaspoon vanilla extract

METHOD

Preheat oven to 350 degrees F (175 degrees C). Grease and flour two 9-inch round pans.

Beat shortening and sugar until light and fluffy. Add eggs one at a time, mixing until fully incorporated. Stir in butter flavoring. Make a paste with food coloring and cocoa and add to the shortening mixture.

Mix buttermilk, salt, baking soda and vinegar; add to batter alternating with the flour mixture.

Divide batter into prepared pans. Bake in preheated oven until cake springs back when touched lightly with a finger or tester comes out clean, 20 to 30 minutes. Cook completely on wire rack.

To Make Cream Cheese Frosting: beat butter and cream cheese with an electric mixer until smooth. Gradually beat in confectioners' sugar and 1 teaspoon vanilla. Mix until well blended.

Almond Cake

By Chef Carl

INGREDIENTS

1 small to medium orange

1 lemon

6 ounces' raw almonds

1 cup all-purpose flour

1 tablespoon baking powder

4 eggs

½ teaspoon salt

1 ½ cups sugar

⅔ cup olive oil

Confectioners' sugar

METHOD

Place the orange and the lemon in a saucepan, and cover with water. Bring to a boil over medium-high heat, then reduce the heat and simmer for 30 minutes. Drain and cool.

Heat the oven to 325 degrees, and set a rack in the middle position. Bake the almonds 10 to 15 minutes. Set aside to cool completely. When the almonds are cool, pulse them in a food processor until ground.

Set oven to 350 degrees, and grease a 9-inch spring form pan.

When the citrus is cool, cut the lemon in half, and discard the pulp and seeds. Cut the orange in half, and discard seeds. Put the fruits in the food processor and process almost to a paste.

In a small bowl, whisk the flour and baking powder. Combine eggs and salt. Beat until foamy. Beat in the sugar. Fold in the flour mixture. Add the citrus, almonds and olive oil, and beat on low speed until incorporated. Pour the batter into the pan, and bake for about 1 hour. Let cool for 10 minutes, unmold and dust with confectioners' sugar.

Amy Ruth's Chocolate Devil's Food Cake

By Chef Carl

INGREDIENTS

Butter and flour for preparing pans

2 ½ cups all-purpose flour

1 teaspoon baking soda

½ teaspoon baking powder

½ teaspoon salt

1 ¼ cups buttermilk

1 teaspoon vanilla extract

11 tablespoons unsalted butter, at room temperature

1 ½ cups sugar

2 large eggs

4 ounces unsweetened chocolate, melted

FOR THE CHOCOLATE FROSTING:

8 cups (2 pounds) sifted confectioners' sugar

1 ⅔ cups unsweetened cocoa powder

½ teaspoon salt

1 ½ cups (3 sticks) unsalted butter, at room temperature

½ cup margarine, at room temperature

¼ cup dark corn syrup

2 tablespoons vanilla extract

¾ cup heavy cream, or as needed

METHOD

Preheat oven to 350 degrees. Butter 3 9-inch round cake pans, and line the bottoms with wax or parchment paper. Lightly butter the paper. Dust pans with flour, and shake out

COOKING UP A CONVERSATION

excess.

Sift together the flour, baking soda, baking powder and salt. In a small bowl, combine buttermilk and vanilla.

In a large bowl, using an electric mixer set at medium-high speed, cream the butter. Slowly add the sugar, and continue beating until well blended and light colored. Add eggs one at a time, beating well after each addition. Add dry ingredients alternately with the buttermilk mixture in 2 or 3 additions, beating well after each addition. Beat in the melted chocolate until well blended. Spoon batter into prepared pans, and smooth tops with a rubber spatula.

Bake for 30 to 35 minutes, or until a toothpick inserted in center of a cake layer comes out clean. Let cake layers cool in the pans on wire racks for 10 minutes, then invert onto other racks and peel off the paper. Invert again, and let cool completely on the racks. Frost with chocolate frosting.

For chocolate frosting: Sift the confectioners' sugar, cocoa and salt together. Using a stand mixer, cream together the butter and margarine on high until light yellow and slightly thickened, about 3 minutes. With mixer still running, add corn syrup and vanilla. Reduce speed to low and add sugar mixture in two batches, beating well after each. Blend in 3/4 cup cream until frosting is a spreading consistency, adding more if needed. Increase speed to high and beat until light and creamy, about 2 minutes more; there will be about 8 cups of frosting. Spoon about 1 cup into a pastry bag fitted with a medium star tip.

For assembly: Using a long serrated knife, cut each cake horizontally into two equal layers. Spread first layer with about a fifth of frosting, then place second layer on top of it and frost it, too. Repeat with third and fourth layers. Frost sides with all remaining frosting except what is in pastry bag. Pat macaroon crunch on sides of cake (not top) until covered. Using frosting in pastry bag, pipe 6 rosettes on top of cake. Serve immediately, or cover and refrigerate, allowing cake to stand at room temperature for about an hour before slicing.

Pecan Pie

By Chef Carl

INGREDIENTS

FOR THE CRUST:

8 ounces' butter, at room temperature

¾ teaspoon salt

2 tablespoons sugar

3 cups flour, sifted

FOR THE FILLING:

- 4 tablespoons unsalted butter, at room temperature
- ½ cup honey, such as clover
- ¼ cup Dark Corn Syrup
- 1 teaspoon vanilla extract
- 1 tablespoon dark rum
- ¼ teaspoon freshly grated nutmeg
- Pinch of salt
- 4 extra-large eggs
- 2 cups shelled pecans

Whipped cream or vanilla ice cream, for serving

METHOD

Mix butter, salt and sugar in a standing mixer on low speed for 1 minute. Add flour and mix on low speed just until ingredients come together. Add 6 tablespoons water and mix only until dough comes together; if it doesn't come together right away, add another tablespoon water. Do not overmix. Scrape mixture out onto a sheet of plastic wrap and flatten into a square. Wrap well and refrigerate overnight.

Very lightly butter a 9-inch pie dish. Divide dough into two equal pieces. Refrigerate one piece while you roll out the other. Ease the dough into the bottom edges of the pan and crimp the top edge. Pierce the bottom in several places with a fork. Refrigerate uncovered for several hours or overnight. (Other dough half may be rolled out and frozen for up to 3 months.)

Heat oven to 325 degrees. Line crust with parchment and fill with pie weights. Place on a baking sheet and bake for 15 minutes. Remove from oven and carefully remove pie weights and parchment. Return crust to oven and bake 15 to 20 minutes, until lightly browned. Let cool completely.

Increase oven temperature to 350 degrees. Cream butter in a standing mixer fitted with the paddle, or in a food processor. Add honey and golden syrup and cream together until smooth. Scrape down bowl and beater. Add vanilla, rum, nutmeg and salt and mix. Add eggs, one at a time, beating each one until incorporated before adding next.

Fill pie shell with pecans and smooth them out to make an even layer. Scrape in butter and egg mixture, using a rubber spatula to scrape the bowl clean. Place on a baking sheet and bake 30 to 35 minutes, until nuts are lightly browned and filling is just about set. The filling will puff up and may be bubbling, but it will settle as it cools. Do not overbake; if you leave it in too long, it will crack. Remove from oven and cool on a rack.

Miss Hodge's West Indian Black Cake

By Chef Carl

INGREDIENTS

2 cups mixed dried fruit (equal parts raisins, currants, prunes and dried cherries)

1 cup Guinness stout

¼ cup muscatel or fruit-flavored brandy

½ to ¾ cup dark West Indian rum (preferably Appleton, Old Oak or Cockspur)

6 ounces' butter

½ cup sugar

2 large or 3 medium eggs

1 teaspoon vanilla extract

¼ teaspoon freshly grated nutmeg

2 tablespoons burnt-sugar coloring (available at West Indian markets; see note)

1 cup flour

1 teaspoon baking powder

METHOD

Place the dried fruit in a glass or ceramic bowl and cover with the Guinness stout, the muscatel or brandy and 1/4 cup of the rum. Cover and refrigerate for at least 3 days (and up to several weeks -- the preferred method). Check the mixture every other day: if the fruit has soaked up all the liquor, add another splash of rum or stout and stir.

Preheat the oven to 350 degrees.

Grind the fruit mixture to a mushy pulp in a blender or food processor. Measure out 2 cups of the mixture and set aside.

In a mixing bowl, cream the butter and sugar. Beat in the eggs one at a time.

Add the vanilla, nutmeg and burnt-sugar coloring; mix well

In another bowl, sift together the flour and baking powder

Add, alternately, the fruit mixture and dry ingredients to the batter, mixing until just incorporated after each addition. Do not beat.

Pour the batter into a 9-by-1 1/2-inch deep round pan and bake for 1 hour to 1 hour and 15 minutes, or until a toothpick inserted in the middle comes out clean.

COOKING UP A CONVERSATION

While the cake is still warm, splash the remaining 1/4 cup of rum over the top. Let cool. The finished cake is quite moist, almost like an English plum pudding. It is at its best when served a day or two after baking, and it will last for two weeks or more if kept in the refrigerator and occasionally topped up with rum.

Vanilla Ice Cream

By Chef Carl

INGREDIENTS

2 cups heavy cream, preferably organic and not ultra-pasteurized

2 cups half-and-half, preferably organic, or 1 cup additional heavy cream plus 1 cup whole milk

½ vanilla bean, split lengthwise and seeds scraped out with the tip of a sharp knife

1 teaspoon pure vanilla extract

1 cup granulated sugar

½ teaspoon salt

METHOD

In a saucepan or a microwave-safe container, combine cream, half-and-half and vanilla bean and seeds (or tea and vanilla extract). On the stove or in the microwave, bring mixture to a simmer. Immediately turn off heat. Add sugar or corn syrup and salt and mix until sugar dissolves, about 1 minute. Taste and add more sugar and salt as needed to balance the flavors. The mixture should taste slightly too sweet when warm; the sweetness will be muted when the ice cream is frozen. Strain mixture into a container and refrigerate until very cold, at least 4 hours and preferably overnight. Churn mixture in an ice cream maker according to manufacturer's instructions. Serve immediately or transfer to an airtight container and let freeze until hard.

Inez Bass' Black Velvet Cake

By Chef Carl

INGREDIENTS

Butter and flour for preparing pans

2 ½ cups all-purpose flour

1 teaspoon baking soda

½ teaspoon baking powder

½ teaspoon salt

1 ¼ cups buttermilk

1 teaspoon vanilla extract

11 tablespoons unsalted butter, at room temperature

1 ½ cups sugar

2 large eggs

4 ounces unsweetened chocolate, melted

FOR THE CHOCOLATE FROSTING

8 cups (2 pounds) sifted confectioners sugar

1 ⅔ cups unsweetened cocoa powder

½ teaspoon salt

1 ½ cups (3 sticks) unsalted butter, at room temperature

½ cup margarine, at room temperature

¼ cup dark corn syrup

2 tablespoons vanilla extract

¾ cup heavy cream, or as needed

COOKING UP A CONVERSATION

METHOD

Preheat oven to 350 degrees. Butter 3 9-inch round cake pans, and line the bottoms with wax or parchment paper. Lightly butter the paper. Dust pans with flour, and shake out excess. Sift together the flour, baking soda, baking powder and salt. In a small bowl, combine buttermilk and vanilla. In a large bowl, using an electric mixer set at medium-high speed, cream the butter. Slowly add the sugar, and continue beating until well blended and light colored. Add eggs one at a time, beating well after each addition. Add dry ingredients alternately with the buttermilk mixture in 2 or 3 additions, beating well after each addition. Beat in the melted chocolate until well blended. Spoon batter into prepared pans, and smooth tops with a rubber spatula. Bake for 30 to 35 minutes, or until a toothpick inserted in center of a cake layer comes out clean. Let cake layers cool in the pans on wire racks for 10 minutes, then invert onto other racks and peel off the paper. Invert again, and let cool completely on the racks. Frost with chocolate frosting.

For chocolate frosting: Sift the confectioners' sugar, cocoa and salt together. Using a stand mixer, cream together the butter and margarine on high until light yellow and slightly thickened, about 3 minutes. With mixer still running, add corn syrup and vanilla. Reduce speed to low and add sugar mixture in two batches, beating well after each. Blend in 3/4 cup cream until frosting is a spreading consistency, adding more if needed. Increase speed to high and beat until light and creamy, about 2 minutes more; there will be about 8 cups of frosting. Spoon about 1 cup into a pastry bag fitted with a medium star tip.

For assembly: Using a long serrated knife, cut each cake horizontally into two equal layers. Spread first layer with about a fifth of frosting, then place second layer on top of it and frost it, too. Repeat with third and fourth layers. Frost sides with all remaining frosting except what is in pastry bag. Pat macaroon crunch on sides of cake (not top) until covered. Using frosting in pastry bag, pipe 6 rosettes on top of cake. Serve immediately, or cover and refrigerate, allowing cake to stand at room temperature for about an hour before slicing.

COOKING UP A CONVERSATION

Cooking with Friends

Chef Carl with Mario Batali & Neicey Nash

Chef Carl & His Mom with Oprah Winfrey

Chef Dana with Phylicia Rashad

Chef Dana with Beverly Crawford

Chef Carl with Morgan Freeman

Chef Carl with Michael Jackson

Chef Dana with Kenny Holliday

Chef Dana with Cheryl Lee Ralph

Chef Carl with Chef Emeril Lagasse

Chef Carl with Sydney Poitier

www.ingramcontent.com/pod-product-compliance
Lightning Source LLC
Chambersburg PA
CBHW080738230426
43665CB00020B/2786